Heavenly Realm Publishing
Houston, Texas

Emphasis within Scripture quotations is the author's own. Please note that LaJohna Newbould capitalizes all pronouns in Scripture that refer to God.

Published by, Heavenly Realm Publishing
PO Box 682532
Houston, TX 77268
1-866-216-0696

Visit our Website at: www.heavenlyrealmpublishing.com

Printed in the United States of America

ISBN—13- 9781937911-95-9 (soft cover)
ISBN—13- 9781937911-96-6 (hard cover)
ISBN—13- 9781937911-30-0 (ebook)

Library of Congress Control Number—2015958986
1. Poetry : Inspirational & Religious: God Things/ 2. POETRY / Women Authors: God Things/ 3. Poetry : General: God Things/ LaJohna Newbould

This book is printed on acid free paper.

GOD

Things

Poetry Book

LaJohna Newbould

DEDICATION

This book is dedicated to God the Father, God the Son and God the Holy Spirit. For They (He) are the inspiration behind every poem written in this book.

GOD THINGS

What is the tapestry of events,
That weaves together the fabric of our lives?
Most people say they are just coincidences,
Not woven together by someone on High.

We travel to and fro,
Thinking we have things well in hand.
Forgetting that everything we say or do,
Is under God's command.

So as we go about our day.
And we give credit to the Lord above,
We find it is in all those little "God Things",
That we are woven together with His love.

TO THE READERS

As with all my books, my focus is on you, the reader. For it is my desire to introduce you to the God that I serve. The living God. The God of the Bible. The one who gave His life so we might live.

I pray you will open your hearts and your minds to the fact that God loves you. Think about it. The God who created the whole universe and everything within it loves you.

TABLE OF CONTENT

TABLE OF CONTENTS

TABLE OF CONTENTS

YOUR LIGHT

I humbly ask Your forgiveness,
For not allowing Your light to shine through.
I humbly ask Your forgiveness,
For not doing all I could do.

For if others cannot see You,
As I walk along the way.
The love You have put inside of me,
I have covered up and betrayed.

I have allowed this world to come in,
And take away the peace You gave to me.
As I walk through the darkness of this valley,
It is Your light in the distance I see.

As I keep heading toward that light,
The pain seems too great to bear,
But I know You are waiting,
My burden with me to share.

So if I fall along the way,
And I struggle to keep You in sight,
May You hold on to me with Your love,
And never give up the fight.

The darkness fights to be triumphant.
The world keeps calling me to come.
But Your light keeps right on shining,
Showing me the way back home.

What blessed peace I receive,
When Your arms I walk into.
Lord, let Your light so shine in me,
I am no longer me, but You.

THE PATH

I look forward to our walk each day,
As I walk along the path with You.
You take my hand and You guide me,
Showing me what and what not to do.

You open my eyes to things up ahead,
Letting me know to be careful here,
Steadily guiding me onward,
Giving me confidence and pushing
    back fear.

The path is open before me,
With all of its cares and woes.
As You and I journey forward,
You prepare the way I am to go.

So step by step I venture on,
Knowing I am safe in Your care.
For You have my back covered,
As I wander here and there.

Thank You, Lord, for allowing me
    the freedom,
To step forward in Your grace.
Knowing You will catch me,
If I fall flat on my face.

The path is open before me,
So take my hand and let's go.
I want to take part in the journey ahead
For it is You I want this world to know.

I AM CONTENT

As I lay in bed just before dawn,
Words keep rhyming in my head.
Sleep holds on to my body,
But I know to get up instead.

"The Garden" is calling out to me,
So I hurry to get outside.
I rush to make things ready,
Before my Savior walks by.

He has come in all His glory,
Wanting to talk for a little while.
I want to make sure I am there,
Just to catch a glimpse of His smile.

I rush to take my seat.
I open my heart and I welcome Him in.
My Savior and I are now One,
Peace flowing from deep within.

I caught Him as He passed by.
I reached out and He took my hand.
I stopped in that wonderful moment,
Knowing Jesus was in full command.

I know I want Him to guide my life,
For He knows much more than I.
And knowing the love He gave for me,
I am content with Him by my side.

MY CHAMPION

The road is long and it stretches before me.
There are valleys along the way.
Your voice keeps calling me onward,
For I have a part in this world to play.

I have started this walk for a reason.
Though the reason, is not now clear.
I will push steadily forward,
Casting out doubt and allowing no fear.

You are the "God of all Creation."
I am so proud to be called Your own.
As I walk through this valley before me,
I know I am not alone.

For You will never leave nor forsake me,
And I know this to be true.
Your Word has stated clearly,
I can put my faith and trust in You.

So as I look at the road before me,
Smooth out the bumps ahead.
Soften the sticks and stones meant to hurt me
And fill me with Your peace instead.

Hold me securely in Your arms,
Shielding me from the arrows that fly.
Letting me know You are "My Champion"
And I can rest safely with You by my side.

THE ONE

I want to walk with You.
I want to talk with You.
I want to hear what You have to say.
So take my hand and guide me and hear
    me as I pray.

Know that I come before You,
Uncovered and alone.
Stand beside me and walk before me,
As I head out into the unknown.

You are the God "In the beginning."
You are the God "At the end."
You are the God "All through the middle."
You are the God "on whom I can depend."

You walk with me through the valleys.
You stand with me on the mountain tops.
You point me in the right direction,
Never allowing me to stop.

Always trudging forward.
Always learning as I go.
Always covered by the blood,
Of the "One" who loves me so.

LEFT BEHIND

The morning has arrived and I am with my God.
My hand He takes in His.
Others are all around me,
Now our lives with Him we will live.

No more calling out to friends and neighbors.
Our family members we will have to let go.
We have made our choice to be with Him.
Now He has called and it is time to go.

My heart breaks for those who are left behind.
My whole being cries at just the thought.
Knowing they had the same chance as I,
But were not willing to follow the One they sought.

I now stand before Him in all His glory,
Just as others must do,
But I am covered by His blood,
And I so pray, you are, too.

THE BLOOD FLOWS FREELY

The garden awaits my coming.
All Heaven takes a breath.
As I accept my Lord and Savior,
And He saves me from eternal death.

I know this has got to be,
A minute taste of Heaven above.
Just being in His presence,
And filled with such overwhelming love.

Now I am covered by the blood,
From mistakes that would take me from Him.
He stepped forward with His mercy,
And took away my sin.

The blood flows freely from the cross.
It covers one and all.
Oh, won't you please answer Him,
When you hear His voice call.

THE IMAGE OF HIS FACE

The garden gate is open wide.
You may enter anytime you please.
His arms are always welcoming.
The truth of His Word He wants you to see.

He wants you to know there is forgiveness
For all the wrong things you have done.
All you have to do is come before Him
Asking to be covered by His shed Blood.

The walk that follows this first step
Will deepen the relationship you have begun.
Now as you step forward,
You are in the palm of God's only Son.

He will walk with you and talk with you
And He will prepare the way.
So as you journey onward,
You will learn something new everyday.

So take a little time just stop and be still.
Hear His voice calling out to you.
Step forward in His mercy and grace
And accept what He wants you to do.

For He knows the truth of all things.
He knows where He wants you to go.
He knows what He wants you to accomplish.
He wants to take care of your soul.

So walk this path with boldness.
Walk this path in His grace.
Walk this path with His love and mercy
Always keeping before you the "Image of His Face."

YOUR TRUTH

I love to meet You at the garden gate.
I love just being with You.
I love the way You open my eyes
As You show me Your Word is true.

The way You take a thought,
As my mind wanders here and there.
Then You settle on a topic.
I listen, then Your Word with me You share.

You open windows and doors,
Not seen by me before.
Your precious Word is before me,
As I walk with my Lord.

Each day the journey continues,
From the dawn to the setting sun.
Wherever this path leads,
It has already begun.

So as we walk together,
You show me which way to go.
And in Your infinite wisdom and mercy,
Allow me Your truth to know.

THE POWER OF YOUR NAME

As we walk the path set before us,
May Your Word be in our hearts.
May Your love and mercy follow us,
Never setting us apart.

May the walk You set before us,
Guide us to Your truth.
May we ever be learning,
And deepening our relationship with You.

For You are the One to whom we are committed.
You are the One to whom we have cast our lot.
You are the God of all Creation.
The One whom our hearts have always sought.

So as we stand before You,
With full armor and ready to go.
Help us to cast away all fear and doubt,
Never allowing them to show.

For our strength comes from You.
It comes in the power of Your name.
As we walk this path before us,
Our lives will never be the same.

BY YOUR SIDE

The wind blows softly through the trees,
Announcing the arrival of my Lord.
Though I know He has never left me,
His presence is stronger than before.

He takes the lead and I follow.
Which way we go I do not care.
All I want is to be with Him,
As His Word, with me, He shares.

He leads me forward through the gate.
We enter as if we are one.
Oh, Holy Ones of Israel,
Your arrival is soon to come.

Open the hearts and minds of Your people.
Allow us to step forward in Your Name.
Let those who do not believe in You,
Realize You are coming again.

You said You would return,
And that time is drawing nigh.
When Heaven's gate will open,
And we will be by Your side.

MY BEST FRIEND

The quiet stillness of the morning,
Is broken by human hands.
But our time together stands firm,
For You are the rock on which I stand.

Louder and louder it gets,
Trying to take me away from You,
But You are the One I seek,
As our walk through the garden begins a new.

The comfort of Your arms surrounds me.
The noise is pushed aside.
My Savior and I continue our walk,
With Him as my only guide.

The world is all around me,
Trying to keep me from entering in.
The walk down the garden pathway,
In the presence of my best friend.

His hand beckons me onward,
And so to Him I go.
Desiring more to be with Him,
Than anyone I know.

BLOOD BOUGHT

As we commit this day to You,
With all its many cares.
We know the road we travel,
Is something we want to share.

For You have prepared the way,
Before we even had the thought.
Now we must step forward,
And give it all we have got.

You are the Savior of the world.
All creation knows Your Name.
Now we stand together,
To let people know You came.

It started with the birth of a babe,
And it ended at the cross.
Now we stand before You,
Ready to go and Blood bought.

What lies ahead is a mystery.
The answer of which we do not know.
But in full confidence we will follow You,
Wherever You want us to go.

YOUR EYES

A thought has flitted across my mind.
One not worthy in the presence of the throne.
One that keeps me from being with You.
The Savior Who has called me His own.

Knowing His great love for me,
Makes me stop in my tracks.
Falling on my knees to ask forgiveness,
I know that before going forward I first must go back.

Our relationship has been interrupted,
But I know I will find forgiveness there.
Though I have broken His heart many times,
I am always welcome as I return to His care.

Father, forgive my step off the path.
Allow me to learn from my mistakes.
Fill me with more love and compassion,
For Your Son died for all our sakes.

There is no sin greater than another.
Through Your eyes all are the same.
The only way they are forgiven,
Is through the power of Jesus' Holy Name.

IN THE ARMS OF MY SAVIOR

I come to the garden alone.
I meet my Savior there.
We walk through the wonders of His Word,
For there is so much, He wants to share.

He wants me to know of His great love.
The love that sent Him to the cross.
The love that required His pain and suffering,
So I would not be lost.

We take a step and as we do,
He explains His Word to me.
Oh, what joy I experience,
As through my Savior's eyes, I see.

Each step we take opens up a new,
The path that lies ahead.
The one that stands before me,
Showing His Word alive and not dead.

For He is the light that guides me.
The One I will follow unto death.
For when He went to the Cross,
He gave, for me, His best.

With His great love before me,
All suffering and shame behind.
I am in the arms of my Savior,
And He is truly mine.

THE STORM CLOUDS
ARE GATHERING

The storm clouds are gathering,
The waves are getting high,
The thunder rolls and the lightning flashes,
And the winds are much more than a sigh.

They tend to overtake us.
They throw us from side to side.
Never caring of the pain they inflict,
Or the panic that rises inside.

The ship seems to be sinking.
Our eyes glance desperately around.
We seek safety from the storm.
A place for our feet on solid ground.

We hear the storm raging around us.
Our eyes see the darkness closing in.
We wonder at this point in time,
If our world is coming to an end.

But then through the darkness we see,
The light of the sun beginning to shine.
We step forward and embrace it,
With a peace that is now yours and mine.

Yes, we did stumble and falter.
Yes, we thought we were going to sink.
But then our Lord put out His hand,
And pulled us back from the brink.

His ways are not our ways,
Sometimes we just do not understand.
Let go of the fear and the panic,
For God really does have a plan.

HIS LAST CALL

Again we meet at the garden gate.
Each day our walk begins a new.
He shows me things I have not seen before.
He blesses me as I step through.

The gate is always open.
Its wonders to behold.
The lessons learned on the other side,
Are each more precious than silver or gold.

Each path holds a different treasure.
When followed, bring such delight.
They open up a whole new world,
In which the Son is the only light.

There is a peace that is found within.
It cannot be measured by any man.
When I went through that garden gate,
I found the rock on which I now stand.

Won't you take that step inside?
It is open to one and all.
Won't you listen for the Savior's voice?
For soon, it will be His last call.

OPEN OUR EYES

Open our eyes, Lord, so we may see,
When we have wronged another.
Open our eyes, Lord, so we may see,
When we have used Your Word as a cover.

Let us know when we are to speak,
Or from our mouths, nothing is to go forth.
Let us hear Your voice, Lord,
For words of our choosing have no worth.

For Your voice is the one we long to hear.
Your word is what we want instilled in our hearts.
Your presence is what we long for.
A relationship filled with love from the start.

Your arms are open wide.
Your face filled with so much love.
We never want to leave Your embrace,
To deal with matters which are not from above.

But our lives are as they are.
We must deal with matters as they come.
Everyday deepening our relationship with,
God the Father, Holy Spirit, and the Son.

PAGE BY PAGE

Our paths are the same as I walk by His side.
With Him teaching me, as we go along.
Opening up the truth of His Word,
And putting into my heart a brand new song.

Sometimes I struggle with what He has shown me.
Sometimes I say, "Lord, how can this be?"
But He takes my hand and we keep right on walking.
A world filled with love for me to see.

Page by page He takes me through the wonders
    of His Word,
Never letting go of my hand.
Bringing to my heart the scriptures,
That allow me to understand.

Onward and onward we go,
Through the valleys and over the hills.
His mysteries unfolding before my eyes,
As this earthly life, becomes quiet and still.

We sit in the calmness of the moment.
My heart reaching out to His.
Feeling the depth of His love for me,
And the peace only He can give.

HEAVENLY SHORE

Hold on to me when the night is lonely.
Hold on to me when the night is long.
Hold on to me when the world assails me.
Hold on to me and make me strong.

For when Your arms surround me,
And I am safe in Your care.
I know that whatever lies ahead,
Is a burden You will share.

You will not leave me to carry it alone.
The brunt of it Your shoulders will bear.
For when You and I became One,
Life's road no longer has the power to scare.

So as our paths are forever entwined,
May I go forward in boldness and faith.
Knowing You will be forever by my side,
And keep me on the path that is narrow and straight.

Your love is all encompassing.
Your grace is so much more.
It allows me the freedom to walk this life,
With my eyes forever on that heavenly shore.

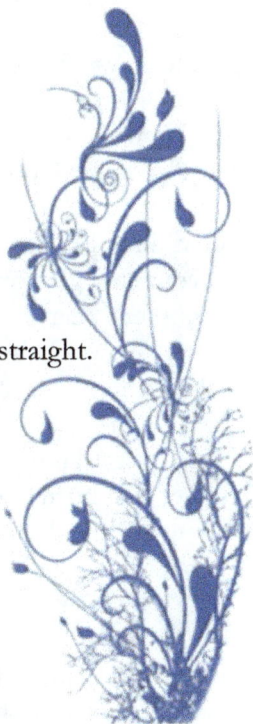

A MOTHER'S LOVE

She did not know what was to come.
All she knew was she was to have a son.
She knew He was special in a Godly way,
But did not know the price He came to pay.

A mother's love kept her close to Him.
Not understanding He would die for all sin.
As a babe, she held Him in her arms.
Holding Him close when life would do Him harm.

As He grew, she pondered in her heart,
The words the angel had spoken at the start.
She knew He would grow to be a man.
She also knew God had a plan.

What that plan was to be?
Never a thought toward Calvary.
A mother's heart broke in two,
When her eyes beheld what her son was going
    through.

Her love for Him took away her breath,
As her first born, faced His death.
Her eyes beheld the storms that day,
As her Son, gave His life away.

She looked at Him with tears a flow.
A mother's heart letting Him go.
Back to the Father from whence He had come.
This babe, this boy, this man, her Son.

HIS EYES

He came to die for all of us.
It was part of His earthly plan.
He came to die for all of us.
To redeem the souls of man.

As a babe, He was born into this world,
To suffer and to die.
As a man, He knew the price He would pay,
For Satan's big lie.

He walked steadily forward,
His eyes never leaving His Father's face.
Knowing what He had to do,
For the redemption of the human race.

Adam had condemned us all to death.
With His death, Jesus brought us life.
His steps always following God's plan,
Though He lived in a world of strife.

As His eyes beheld the cross,
And all the pain and suffering He would bear.
He stumbled for just a moment,
As He entered the lion's lair.

But God is God, the great "I Am."
His Word forever true.
He stepped forward in His love,
And chose to die for me and you.

BEAUTIFUL GIFT

As I sit by the tree in all its splendor,
I gaze at the nail hanging there.
It reminds me of the fate of the One,
Whose life I chose to share.

At this time of the year we celebrate His birth.
Sometimes we forget why He came.
The nail hangs there as a silent reminder,
Of His death and our shame.

As a babe, He nursed from His mother's breast.
As a child, He walked and talked and played.
As a man, He went to the cross.
As a Savior, our souls He saved.

I stare at the nail and it brings to mind,
The great love my Savior has for me.
That He was willing to leave Heaven for earth,
And to suffer such agony.

The Christmas tree shows the beauty of His birth,
The nail shows the agony of His death.
As a babe, He was welcomed into His
      mother's arms.
As a son, His Father welcomed Him as He
      breathed His last breath.

Oh, what a beautiful gift we received,
When God sent forth His son.
Oh, what a beautiful gift was given,
When Jesus fought Satan and won.

MY NEED

I come to the garden alone.
I humbly ask You to meet me there.
Knowing You are the One I can count on.
The One on whom I can cast my cares.

My eyes seek Yours for reassurance.
The burden I carry weighing me down.
I know You are out there somewhere.
My eyes search, but You cannot be found.

I feel You have deserted me.
I feel so lost and alone.
As I desperately seek Your guidance,
My heart tells me to keep holding on.

I have reached the point where all seems lost.
My soul cries out in agony "Why?"
My Savior wraps His arms around me,
And He just lets me cry.

For I have reached rock bottom.
I am willing to go wherever He may lead.
It is no longer my will I seek.
It is into His hands I cast my need.

TRUST

Oh, Lord, my God I have come so far.
When on You, I first cast my need.
On that day when I first decided,
It was in Your hands I would fail or succeed.

I stood at the entrance to the garden.
The stakes I nailed into the ground.
A whole new world opened up before me
As Your path before me, I found.

Each day our relationship grew stronger.
I found I could trust You with me.
I found comfort in Your caring and strength
And with You is where I wanted to be.

Each step we have taken together
Has caused excitement and sometimes fear,
But through it all I have noticed,
Your presence has always been near.

You have walked and talked and guided me
Every step of the way.
Patiently showing me the depth of Your love
And that Your love is here to stay.

IT IS IN HIM

A new path has opened up before me.
I know not where it will go.
All I know is the gate is open
So I go in search of my Lord.

There is no magic potion
I can call on to set me straight.
I simply step forward in love and trust
In Jesus placing all of my faith

Now no matter where I go
Each step I take belongs to Him.
He is the One I have chosen to follow.
He is the One who paid the price for my sin.

So it is in Him I step through the gate.
It is in Him I walk down the path.
It is in Him I never give up.
It is in Him I finish my task.

ONE DAY

Thank You, Lord, for holding on to me,
Though the things I did were not right.
Thank You for looking through my sin,
And holding my hand so tight.

Thank You for looking past the words and deeds,
Though Your heart ached with the pain.
You just kept holding on to my hand,
Hoping to cleanse me of my shame.

Day after day You called out to me,
Wanting to cleanse me as white as snow.
Each day I chose to wallow in my sin,
Refusing its ugliness to let go.

Ever so patient, loving and kind,
When blow after blow You received.
All because in the depth of my sin,
I chose not to believe.

But then one day You called.
I heard Your voice loud and clear.
I no longer wanted to run and hide.
By Your side I just wanted to be near.

A NAIL SCARRED HAND

I stand at the garden gate,
Not knowing which way to go.
Do I want to enter in?
Or do I want to go on as before?

I stand there completely helpless,
Seeing the purity of no sin beyond.
Wanting so much to enter in.
Wanting all my sin to be gone.

What I had done loomed before me,
Causing me to think I was too late,
Causing me to hang my head in shame,
Not wanting to see the reality of my fate.

I stand looking at those on the other side,
Hoping someone will call out to me.
I stare at them with jealous eyes,
Trying to cope with the pain others cannot see.

How I long to take that step,
To be free of the sin weighing me down.
How do you put your life in the hand of someone,
You have denied up until now?

As I stand there so alone and confused,
A nail scarred hand I see.
Then a face filled with so much love and
    compassion,
I cannot help, but fall on my knees.

In that moment I know I am forgiven,
Knowing now a choice I must make.
So placing my hand in His,
I walk through the garden gate.

I AM FREE

Lord, I hear Your voice in the morning.
I hear Your voice throughout the day.
I hear Your voice during the nighttime.
Yearning for You to show me the way.

I stand before You in wonder and awe,
Seeing the love and compassion in Your eyes.
Knowing I am not worthy to touch You,
As Your hand beckons me to Your side.

I tentatively reach out to take Your hand,
Knowing the darkness in my soul,
But You reach out with a firm but gentle grip,
Cleansing this body as white as snow.

I no longer fear coming into Your presence.
I no longer fear walking by Your side.
I no longer fear when I make a mistake,
That You will cast me aside.

I am free to learn and to grow and to love.
I am free to walk this earth with no shame.
I am free to be who You want me to be,
All by the power of Jesus' Name.

THAT OLD STUMP

That old stump is there in the garden.
You go around it each and every day.
As long as it stays in the garden,
It will always be in your way.

It is there, it is big and it is annoying.
It cannot easily be plucked out.
It determines the direction you take,
Causing you to sometimes just turn about.

It's roots are deep and it seems too much trouble,
To move it out of the way.
So you continue to tip toe around it,
Day, after day, after day.

Going forward has all but stopped.
You avoid the garden and all that needs done.
You let that big old stump,
Make you turn around and run.

Today you make a decision.
That old stump has dictated your direction far
  too long.
So now, whatever it takes,
Today that old stump will be gone.

Sin is like that old stump.
It stands between you and your goal.
It wants you to give up and leave it there,
Allowing it to eat at your soul.

But once that old stump is removed
There is a peace that settles from within.
Now you are free to go forward
For with Jesus on your side, you will achieve your goal
   in the end.

IN YOUR DARKEST HOUR

Though the storm rages about you,
And fear threatens to take your hand.
Remember there is a God in Heaven,
And it is on His Word that you stand.

He will hold you in your darkest hour.
He will never leave your side.
Though times may get a little tough,
Remember it is in Him that you abide.

Though you may not know what lies ahead,
You know the One in charge of your tomorrows.
So seek the face of the One who loves you,
And give Him all your sorrow.

Stand firm in the face of darkness.
Let nothing stand in your way.
Seek the light at the end of the tunnel.
Get down on your knees and pray.

WITH THIS RING

I have chosen You to be my God.
I have given my life into Your hands.
I have accepted the price You paid for me,
And now beside You I will stand.

I have given into Your care,
All I am or ever hope to be.
For it is You, I have chosen to be with.
It is through You, I am now forever free.

I have chosen to walk by Your side
Come whatever may.
You are the husband of my choice.
I will follow You till my dying day.

As I walk down the aisle,
I am consumed by my love for You.
Each step I take toward the altar,
Opens the door to a life all fresh and new.

The final moment has arrived.
The words "I Do" need to be said.
In that moment I give You my life,
As I say, "With this ring, I Thee wed."

THAT DAY

Travel the road placed before you.
Keep your eyes focused straight ahead.
For the God of all creation,
Placed Himself on the Cross in your stead.

He knows all there is to know,
About you and the life you have lived.
There is not one single thing you can hide,
From the One who chose His life to give.

He weighed in the balance all you had done.
He knew ahead of time all you would do.
But even knowing all of this,
He chose to give His life for you.

Each time the whip touched His back.
Each time a fist found its mark.
Each time the cry "crucify Him" rang out.
The sound tore deep into His heart.

Through it all, He stood fast.
Taking all that came His way.
For He knew the end result,
When He cried "it is finished" that day.

DAUGHTER, I UNDERSTAND

Lord, I brought nothing to the table when
    You called me.
I was not even worth the price You paid.
But when You stepped in and saved me,
What a difference in my life You made.

I may fall from time to time,
And when I do, my heart breaks so.
But I have faith in the One who saved me,
Knowing You will not let me go.

So though I may make mistakes,
You never let go of my hand.
You simply look me in the eye and say,
"Daughter, I understand."

Your eyes speak of Your deep love.
Your embrace comforts my soul.
I simply let You hold me,
As these earthly sorrows, I just let go.

MY CHILD

I heard you in the midnight hour,
As your voice cried out to Me.
I saw you as you sought My face,
As you fell on bended knee.

I heard your cries as you wondered why,
Things around you were not the same.
I listened as you gave them to Me,
And into the power of My Name.

Day by day you came closer to Me.
Day by day you sought My embrace,
And now, My child, as I hold you close,
There is nothing you cannot face.

Just rest in the shelter of My arms.
I will take care of the road ahead.
For you, My child, belong to Me.
There is nothing for you to dread.

A SWEET SPIRIT

You see the clouds in the distance.
You wonder how bad this storm will be.
You stand and watch as it comes closer.
The difference in the sky you see.

You stand and you continue to watch.
The closer it comes the worse it gets.
You watch as it begins to swirl around you.
Its depth you know not yet.

Though its strength continues to grow,
Its source to you unknown.
Its darkness circling around you.
Its fierceness continuing its groan.

As the storm grows in strength,
A sweet spirit settles into your soul.
You know that whatever you face,
Jesus will never let you go.

THE CROSS

The valley stretches before me,
As far as my eyes can see.
I hesitate at its entrance,
What is beyond is unknown to me.

I stare into the darkness,
Not wanting to take that final step.
But decisions have to be made,
And there are times I feel so inept.

But I have a God who understands me.
He knows what I am going through.
He knows just how to handle the matter.
He knows what I need to do.

As I place my hand in His,
A light in the distance I see.
Then in the midst I see a cross,
Knowing the Blood shed there was for me.

In trust I now go forward,
Never letting the Cross leave my sight.
For it is in the Cross that stands before me,
I was given back my life.

RESURRECTION DAY

Be still and know that I am God.
Be still and know that I care.
Be still and know that in your darkest hour,
I will always be there.

For I loved you in the beginning.
I will love you in the end.
I will not take My love from you,
Though you be deep in sin.

The Cross was placed before you.
I could not leave you there.
You could not carry its burden.
Its load too much to bear.

So I placed it on My shoulders.
I carried it all the way.
Now you share in its victory,
With the dawning of resurrection day.

LET GO AND LET GOD

Before the world gets hold of your day,
Give it to the Lord.
Before the world has begun to have its say,
Give it to the Lord.

With Him in charge you will have the peace,
Only He can give.
Step by step He will show you the way,
In which He would have you to live.

His path brings such comfort,
For you know He is looking out for you.
It is in His hands you are always safe,
As each trial ahead confronts you.

With all your strength hold on.
Never, ever letting go.
It is in your weakest moment,
His love, for you, He will show.

Know this if you know anything at all.
Jesus went to the Cross just for you.
So place your life into His hands.
Let go and let God; His will to do.

JUDGEMENT DAY

As you place your hand in Mine,
The responsibility of your care belongs to Me.
If My death is what is required,
I will do it because of My love for thee.

Though I came to share My love with you.
My love you chose not to share.
I showed you the most wonderful things,
But you chose not to care.

So now I sit here waiting,
For you to make up your mind.
I refuse to give up on you,
Until that final moment in time.

That time is fast approaching,
And this I can do nothing about.
For I do the will of My Father,
Until the angel gives one last shout.

Then I will come as was foretold,
And you will no longer be given a choice.
Judgment day has arrived,
And My people know My voice.

GOD'S PLAN

As I go this way or that in the garden,
I realize it is all part of God's plan.
As I travel each path before me,
He strengthens the ground on which I stand.

I may think I have taken a wrong turn,
When things don't come out just right.
Then I see that along the way,
I have never been out of God's sight.

The mistakes I make He has allowed me to make,
So I will learn right from wrong.
His strength guides me through the maze of hurt.
It is in Him I learn to be strong.

Our walk through the garden I would not change,
I have learned so much traveling there.
A burden is so much easier to carry,
If you have someone with whom you can share.

So approach the garden with confidence.
There is nothing you have to handle alone.
Step through the gate provided for you,
Allowing God to introduce you to His Son.

THAT OLD WALL

I stare at the wall in front of me.
It blocks the direction I am to take.
I search for a way around it.
I know what is at stake.

I can see the path on the other side,
Knowing I must get through.
I just don't know how to accomplish it,
For I have already given everything to You.

I search for the answer, but my mind is blank.
I go to the wall and I cry.
The wall still stands and it bars my way,
But my love for You I cannot deny.

So I back up and stare at the wall,
Wondering what it is I need to learn.
Then I give the wall to Jesus,
And now it is no longer my concern.

For, my Lord, He loves me.
I know this from the depth of my heart.
When the appropriate time has arrived,
That old wall will have to depart.

YOUR DIRECTION

Lord, as I travel this path placed before me,
I am never sure which way to turn.
I just place one foot in front of the other,
Knowing it is Your presence for which I yearn.

I trust You with the final direction.
I place in You complete control.
It is in Your hands I will find peace.
It is in You I place the care of my soul.

The path we take may not be of my choice,
But it is the one that has been placed ahead.
Though I would rather seek another direction,
It is by You I am led.

For You are the God who created all things,
And it is Your direction I seek.
I learn so much in the valleys,
But I strive for the mountain peaks.

Why do things happen as they do?
This I do not know.
As You and I go forward,
I know Your truth, to me, You will show.

LORD, HE KNOWS

Someone is out there, Lord,
He is choosing not to follow Your way.
Allowing His circumstances to pull him under,
Thinking that in this he has no say.

Lord, he knows that You love him.
He knows You are with him through times
   good and bad.
He seeks to hold on to his will.
That direction making him sad.

He knows You walk by his side.
You have made Your presence known many times.
Still he chooses the direction he takes,
Without You to keep him in line.

He seeks the world and all it holds,
Insisting he can do it on his own.
Each day pulling him further away from You,
Becoming more and more alone.

Lord, You tapped him on the shoulder
   many years ago.
You let him know his life was blessed.
Now let him know to seek Your face,
And You will do all the rest.

INDECISION

Lord, someone out there is hurting.
He does not know which way to turn.
The world promises him one thing,
But it is Your direction for which he yearns.

He is pulled apart as he stands still.
His indecision making him weak.
Anger and hurt consume him,
As he refuses, Your face, to seek.

He blames each outcome on others,
Forgetting each choice made was his alone.
For he forgot to seek Your face,
Before heading out into the unknown.

Though mistakes were made along the way,
His heart still cries out for You.
So won't You take hold of his hand,
And show him what You can do.

THE RICHES

You have stepped through the entrance to the garden.
You behold the fullness therein.
Your eyes behold the beauty of a life,
Filled with love and no sin.

Then you stop and look around you.
Your unworthiness making itself known.
Fear has stopped you in your tracks,
Taking from you what God has just shone.

You stand in complete awe,
Of what lies down the road ahead.
You stand frozen at the entrance,
Fearing to go forward instead.

God is a God of love.
He knows you will stumble and fall.
All He requires is that you never give up,
But that you give the road ahead your all.

He does not want you to stand still.
He wants you to travel beyond the garden gate.
He wants you to taste of the fullness therein.
He wants all your fears to alleviate.

The fullness of the garden awaits you.
Step by step He calls you to enter in.
As you travel down each pathway,
Your relationship will deepen with Him.

Oh, the riches that lie before you.
He wants you to partake of each one.
He wants you to cast away each fear,
And trust in His only begotten Son.

HE HEARS

Put one foot in front of the other,
As each day you go forth.
Knowing that God loves you,
And in you he finds treasured worth.

He created you out of nothing.
He formed you from the earth's ground.
He breathed into you His Spirit,
Where love can always be found.

Though you may travel a difficult road,
His Spirit within you abides.
He will never set you adrift,
Or allow this world to cast you aside.

He sees you as you walk the path,
Of this world and all it holds.
He hears your heart as it cries out,
Seeking to come in from out of the cold.

He knows you and He loves you.
This you must always remember.
It is in the death of His Son,
He allows you Heaven's gate to enter.

BEING TRUE

The day is before you; embrace it.
Go forth and see what it holds.
Put your hand in the hand of the Shepherd,
As He welcomes you into His fold.

If you stray, He will find you.
If you stumble, He will pick you up.
If you make a wrong turn, He will guide you.
It is at His table you have chosen to sup.

He will hold you in His arms as you cry.
He will cheer you on through times dark and grim.
He will be with you when you reach the mountain top,
As you put your trust in Him.

So take His hand as you go forward.
Putting love before anything else.
Judging not those around you,
Being true to Him first; then to yourself.

LIFE'S JOURNEY

That mountain that looms up ahead.
The one that reaches clear out of sight.
The one that fills your heart with dread.
The one that blocks out all light.

That mountain, My child, is like all the others.
In life's journey it is a stepping stone.
Each time you go forward to reach the peak,
You get closer to God's Heavenly throne.

When you reach the top of that mountain,
There is a valley far below.
It is cold, it is dark, and it is lonely,
But in the distance you can still see your goal.

Sometimes when you reach that mountain top,
The one on the other side is higher than you
    could ever imagine.
But your goal still lies in the distance,
Though you can no longer see it on the horizon.

I will be with you each step of the way,
As you place one foot in front of the other.
For though this world may have its ups
    and downs,
There is much in this life for you to discover.

CHILDREN OF THE KING

We each have a different road to follow.
We each have a different dream.
For God has placed in the depths of our hearts,
A love to which we can cling.

We are to climb every mountain.
We are to travel through each valley below.
We are never, ever to give up,
Though this life has dealt us a blow.

We are the children of the King.
He holds us in the palm of His hand.
There is nothing this world can do to us,
That has not been placed under His command.

So take your rightful place.
Our Savior died for all sin and strife.
Accept His crown of salvation,
Allowing Him to enter your name in the
        Book of Life.

STOP

There is a spiritual and physical side,
To everything that takes place in this world.
There is a battle going on,
For the hearts and minds of each boy and girl.

Those who do not know You,
Know not how the battle will end.
Those who know of Your great love,
Know what the message the Cross did send.

There is life on the other side.
Death cannot keep you in its grasp.
As you go forward in this fight,
You must be aware of Satan's traps.

He will set snares along the way.
He will rejoice when you fall.
But as the Word of God says,
Jesus will catch you if you just call.

For in this world you will have trouble,
Caused by the fall of man.
But you can always count on Jesus,
To lend a helping hand.

So stop and take this moment.
Get down on your knees and pray.
Allow the God of all creation,
To send Satan on his way.

ETCHED IN STONE

As we look around and see our children,
Each one running here and there.
We watch them as they play,
Seeming not to have one care.

We keep that memory in our minds,
For far too soon they will be gone.
They insist on growing up.
So we let them grow, but teach them to be strong.

We hold them in our arms as babes.
We walk beside them as they grow.
Each time they get a little bigger,
Thinking this old world they know.

Year by year their birthdays proclaim,
Just how much time has passed.
Year by year we wonder where time has gone.
Why a little longer it could not last.

We want to hold on and protect them.
They want to grow up and be on their own.
We want to fight their battles for them,
As they charge out into the unknown.

We hold them when they cry.
We laugh with them when they are filled
    with delight.
We stand by their side when they are in trouble,
But allow them to handle each fight.

For as their parents, we gave them life.
We must teach them we will never leave them alone.
Look around you, my child, when times get tough,
Our love for you is etched in stone.

THE ANSWER

When the path ahead is lonely, dark, and cold,
And I don't know which way to turn.
When the trials of each day,
Take away the peace for which I yearn.

I simply walk into my Savior's arms.
I snuggle down into the warmth of His embrace.
I allow His love to encompass me
Knowing this is where I am safe.

So as the evils of this world, surround me.
And right or wrong choices have to be made.
Black and white answers seem to be lost
Becoming a mottled gray.

I go to His Word in confidence.
Knowing the answer I will find there.
No matter what the question.
The answer is found in prayer.

W H Y ?

In the stillness of the night
As I lay across the bed.
So many thoughts clamor
For space within my head.

The house is completely quiet
And I lay there all alone.
I spend some special time with
The Father and His son.

The silence closes in
And everything grows still.
And I think about the One who carried
A Cross to Calvary's Hill.

I picture the mighty angels
Standing at heaven's door.
Pushing and shoving and wanting
To save our Lord.

"Why?" asked the angels.
"Won't You let us rescue Your Son?"
"The battle I sent Him to fight," God answered.
"Has not yet been won."

The angels stood in silence,
Waiting for what was to be.
Until the Father said "It is time,
Bring My Son home to Me."

"The battle has been fought."
"The battle has been won."
"All praise, honor, and glory
Now belong to My Son."

I AM THANKFUL

Lord, it is so nice to be able to talk to You.
To tell You what is happening or what I am going through.
Even though I know You know all of this,
It feels so good to get it off my chest.

Sometimes I talk, sometimes I cry,
But I always know You are by my side.
My walk with You has come such a long way,
Since I found You on that very first day.

Each step I have taken has brought me closer to You.
It thrills my heart completely through.
When I take a step in the wrong direction,
It makes me weep because I was taken in
        by deception.

My heart is so full of my love for You.
I am thankful You have forgiven me for the
        wrong things I do.
I am grateful for You always being there.
My life, my soul, I give into Your care.

FORGIVENESS

In this old life there are things that happen.
Your heart may be filled with despair.
Your mind cannot think because of the pain.
All that was is no longer there.

You look at the road that stretches before you.
You search for just a tiny bit of hope,
But Satan has you in his grasp,
And it is so very hard to cope.

Your pain has been placed for all the world to see.
It makes it so hard to see any light.
If you keep searching for the answers,
God will see and hear your plight.

Forgiveness is in your hands.
It matters not what others may do.
It depends on the depth of your love,
And whether your commitment was made
    in truth.

So go to the throne of God.
Place all your pain and hopelessness there.
Allow Him to work on your behalf,
While you rest in His infinite care.

MY JOURNEY

Lord, Your Word says You will give us the desires of
    our heart,
But my heart I have already given to You.
All I ask is for You to show me the direction,
Giving me the strength for whatever You would have
    me do.

As I place the me that I am, into Your hands.
I await the me You want me to be.
Though the road traveled has been long,
I know You have always walked beside me.

Each path we have taken has had a purpose,
Though I did not always understand.
I knew that Your love surrounded me,
As I struggled to find Your plan.

Though I have not reached the end of my journey,
I treasure each and every moment we have shared.
For it was in those wonderful moments,
I found out just how much You cared.

OUR GIFT FROM GOD

Amidst all the glitz and the glitter,
Amidst all the lights that so brightly shine,
Amidst all the garland and decorations,
And the gifts under the tree that are mine.

Amidst all the hustle and bustle,
Amidst all the songs sang with great cheer,
Amidst all the hugs and the greetings,
The reason for this season is clear.

For long ago, a babe was born in Bethlehem,
In a manger dark and cold.
He was wrapped in swaddling clothes by His mother,
The Bible tells us so.

The wise men followed a star to find Him,
Traveling many miles in their search.
When they beheld this little one,
On Him they lavished gifts of great worth.

So amid all that takes place during the Christmas
    season,
Don't forget this child and why He came.
For He is the reason we celebrate,
Our gift from God and Jesus is His Name.

THIS ONE

When we call on the Name of Jesus,
When we come to Him on bended knee,
He forgives us of our sin.
For He walked this world just as we.

He sees each and every misdeed.
There is not one we can hide from Him.
Our life is an open book.
Its dirtiness revealed on the pages within.

He sees each and every word written.
It hurts Him to see the things we do.
He still looks down on us with love,
As this world each day we walk through.

Why does this Savior of mine love me?
Indeed, I do not know.
I am just so very thankful,
His love cleanses me white as snow.

As each page of my life is written,
As Satan shows it to the Father and says,
    "Look, see,"
Jesus takes the page and erases all that is within,
Saying, "This one belongs to Me."

THE BOOK

The Word of the Lord is so special.
Each Word speaks directly to you.
It is in these Words He tells of His love,
And the reason the Cross was something He
    had to do.

As you walk with Him through each page,
His Words leap out as He takes your hand.
He shows you how much He loves you,
As you travel toward the promise land.

As you read the Word He has placed in your heart,
Allow Him to take you where He will.
It is in that Word He will teach you,
How He commanded the waters to be still.

His love surrounds you as you turn each page,
And with each page He gives you the choice.
To follow the Word He is showing you,
Or to listen to another voice.

The power of His Word belongs to you,
And you belong to Him.
For long ago when He purchased the Book,
He knew how the story would end.

THE LIGHT

The seasons of our lives come and go.
The days pass swiftly one by one.
I try to see my way clear,
With the light from the dawning of the sun.

The light has called me from the darkness.
It has opened my eyes so I can see.
It has called me to taste of its goodness.
Allowing Jesus to reign within me.

Its brightness surrounds me and I enjoy its warmth.
I want to complete every task.
I don't ever want this light to leave,
And I know all I have to do is ask.

I have chosen the light and all that lies within.
From darkness I have chosen to flee.
It is in the brightness of that light,
I will walk through all eternity.

I KNEW

As I stood at the foot of the Cross,
My mind's eye seeing what had taken place.
Standing there in complete denial,
That I had played a part in this man's fate.

How could anyone say I was the reason,
For this visage that no longer looked like a man.
That as the blood ran from His body,
That I, in anyway had a hand.

I stared as His eyes searched the crowd.
Wondering what it was He was so determined to see.
Then as His eyes looked deep into mine,
I knew He had been searching for me.

As Jesus hung there in silence,
My eyes He would not let go.
As His life left His body,
I knew He had just saved my soul.

HIS HEART

When you go to the Lord in prayer,
Take yourself away from everyone.
Remove yourself to your own little space,
So His heart and yours can become one.

Quiet down and listen only to His voice.
Go to Him on bended knee.
Put aside all the advice of family and friends,
Allowing only Him to speak to thee.

Whether you are telling Him how much you love Him,
Or about a problem that lies up ahead.
It is His heart and yours coming together,
That allows Him to say what needs to be said.

In the quietness of that moment,
His heart has reached out and touched yours.
Now as you journey forward,
Of His love you can always be sure.

GOD'S LOVE SONG

As I pass through the entrance of the garden,
I behold what lies beyond.
There is no greater beauty on this earth,
Than the beauty of "God's love song."

I close my eyes and I listen,
As the wind blows through the trees.
It swirls through my hair and caresses my cheek,
And through His eyes, He allows me to see.

He tells me of His great love,
All the while holding my hand.
He shows me the path that lies before me,
As my feet enjoy the coolness of the sand.

My eyes search the garden from the east to
    the west,
Beholding all that is contained within.
Love wells up inside of me,
And I know I just want to be with Him.

With my hand in His I step forward,
Leaving the safety of the garden gate,
But knowing Jesus will walk by my side,
As I step forward to meet my fate.

FEED MY CHILDREN

Feed My children, Oh, My beloved.
Keep them from straying from Me so far.
Show them the love and mercy shown you,
By the One born under the Bethlehem star.

He has called them just like He called you.
He finds no difference between you and them.
His forgiveness lies at the foot of the cross,
Where He took away "all" sin.

He looks at us through eyes of love,
As tears flow freely down His cheeks.
He sees how we struggle from day to day,
As His path, we continually seek.

Feed My children, Oh, My beloved.
But to feed; you first must eat.
Fill yourself full of the Holy Spirit,
Then go forth in Jesus' Name and teach.

SATAN'S LURE

This life will have its problems,
Of this you can be sure.
As evil besets you on every side,
Do not take hold of Satan's lure.

For he will come to you in your darkest moment,
When you are defenseless and alone.
He will tell you things that are untrue,
Seeking to take you as his own.

As Christians we know who Satan is,
We know he is the father of all lies.
Now we must tell all who will listen,
So their souls will live and not die.

BENDED KNEE

Your altar stands before me.
I get down on my knees and pray.
Your love surrounds me as You listen,
To what I have to say.

How blessed I am,
To have such a Savior as You.
For as You walked this world,
You suffered the same as I do.

Each step I take You have already taken.
You know the pitfalls that lie up ahead.
If I would just listen to Your voice,
I could avoid so much fear and dread.

You are my God and I love You.
You are the One I want to please.
Help me, Lord, to do Your bidding,
As I come to You on bended knee.

OUR THOUGHTS

Satan has come to destroy our lives.
In this his aim is to succeed.
Though he tries many different ways,
If you belong to Jesus, to fear there is no need.

For our God is God and there is none other.
All Satan's plans will come to naught.
If we just stay in God's presence,
And on Him we keep our thoughts.

THE STORM

I woke up this morning and the weather was just fine.
I soon realized there was a storm brewing.
I looked around and the signs were all there.
The clouds in the distance were stewing.

Before it hit it was quiet and still.
All of nature was holding its breath.
Then just before the storm arrived,
The Heavens became as still as death.

I sat and I waited for its arrival,
Not knowing how bad it would be.
I just knew that when it arrived,
Its fierceness would be wild and mean.

After the storm was over,
In its path it left nothing but destruction.
Now is the time for rebuilding,
If the pieces can be found for construction.

You look around in wonder,
At what the fierceness of the storm could do.
But then, you simply pick up the pieces,
And allow God to help you through.

THE FULLNESS OF TIME

"My God, My God, why hast Thou forsaken Me?"
Was the cry heard from the Cross.
Those that heard Him say those words,
Knew not what those words had cost.

The fullness of time, for Him, had arrived.
Separation from the Father was now required.
Oh! the pain our Lord suffered,
As Satan pulled Him deep in the mire.

But on resurrection morning, Satan had to let go,
For our Heavenly Father had a plan.
Jesus had entrusted His life to the Father.
Now we entrust our lives into Jesus' hand.

THE PROMISE LAND

Lord, I don't want to be a halfway Christian.
I want to freely give You my all.
I want to be able to rush out and meet You,
When I hear Your voice call.

I want to know when I stand before You,
What You require of me?
I want to know the extent of Your love,
And the price You paid so I could be free.

I want to know that I am forgiven.
That You have come to take my hand.
That together You and I will travel,
Toward "The Promise Land."

We have traveled many roads together.
I have fallen, but You have always picked me up.
As this earthly journey comes to an end,
I know it is at Your table I will sup.

You and I have had our problems.
At times I have fought to have my own way,
But now I gladly give all things into Your hands,
For it is with You I have come to stay.

JUST BEING YOU

Time has passed; years have gone by,
Lines now cover my face.
I no longer see the girl of my youth.
This old lady has taken her place.

Do I wish I could be young again?
Never in a million years.
For with that youth came all those decisions,
That have caused so many tears.

As I look back at the past,
I can see I always made it through.
For no matter what life threw at me,
You were there "Just Being You."

You loved me before I loved You.
You walked by my side before I knew You
      were there.
You called my name before I knew You existed.
You died for me before I even knew You cared.

HOW DO I

Lord, how do I explain Your existence,
To someone who does not believe?
How do I tell them You are alive and well,
Even though You cannot be seen?

How do I tell of Your love and mercy,
When they see all the suffering and wonder why?
How do I make them understand You created all things?
From the depths of the ocean, to the clouds in the sky.

How do I tell them You went to the Cross,
To pay a debt You did not owe?
How do I explain the depth of Your love,
And the truths the Bible has shown?

How do I explain why I follow You,
When they look at me and see my flaws?
How do I explain how You pick me up,
Each and every time I fall?

As I think about all these questions,
I realize it is not up to me.
For it is not in my power,
To take down the wall that allows them to see.

MY HOPE

Thou hast heard my voice in the wilderness,
As I cry out for You to make Your presence known.
I know You hear me as I fall to my knees,
For Your Word tells me, I am not alone.

As I bow to You in complete surrender,
Your love surrounds me like a cloak.
I know You know the truth of all things.
It is in You I place my hope.

MASTER OF MY FATE

Oh, Holy Ones of Israel.
I give this day to You.
Prepare the way before me,
So I will know what to do.

It is You who knows the direction.
It is You who knows the path.
It is You I choose to follow.
It is to You I pledge my troth.

As each day begins a new,
There is so much to learn and to see.
Open my eyes and take my hand,
As a world of possibilities open up to me.

You are the master of my fate.
I choose to give complete control to You.
For though there are choices I must make,
Allow me to see what You would have me do.

For I know that You love me,
And You will stay by my side.
As we travel this day together,
It is in You I choose to abide.

LITTLE LOST SHEEP

Poor little sheep you have lost your way,
Thinking God has deserted you in your hour of need,
But you must know for He has shown you before,
It is not Him, but you that leaves.

He watched as you chose the world and all it holds.
The tears flowing gently down His cheeks.
Then every moment of every day the good Shepherd
  called your name,
But He was no longer the one you chose to seek.

Satan had reared his ugly head,
Telling you lies and the things you wanted to hear.
You no longer listened to that small voice inside,
Turning away from the One who held you so dear.

Then one morning the angels began to sing,
And all of Heaven began to rejoice.
For during the night when evil abounds,
That little lost sheep heard his name called
    and followed the Good Shepherd's voice.

AGAINST ALL ODDS

I am a walking miracle,
For I was made by God.
The Lord of all the universe,
Gave to my birth a nod.

He saw me through eyes of love,
Knowing the mistakes I would make.
But decided to take a chance on me,
Though He knew His heart, I would break.

He stood fast in His love,
As I fell time after time.
Never giving up on me,
Though I repaid Him not in kind.

His love for me never wavered.
He stood fast against all odds.
He went to the Cross at Calvary,
Proclaiming His love as my God.

CHRIST IS OUR FOCUS

Time erodes mind, body and soul
And Satan bears down with a heavy, heavy load.
At times all seems lost and out of place
And we fear it is not possible to win this race.

Life rushes on before our eyes
And we struggle onward looking for the prize.
We cling to the light for the strength to endure
As our own fades and becomes unsure.

Christ is our focus and the reason for life
And our troubles here only sweeten the prize.
As we look to Heaven for His saving grace,
We're reminded that life is a very short race.

When at last we reach the end,
And our hearts cry out free from sin.
Now we walk the streets of gold,
With no more pain or heavy load.

Our friends and family will miss us for a time,
But only until they reach the end of the line.
Then we'll all walk hand in hand
With Jesus through the Promised Land.

*by: **Timmy Lambright***

In Memory of
STELLA PARTEN

MY BEST FRIEND

Stella's headstone arrives today,
But in truth I know she is not there.
For the moment You called her home,
This earthly body she no longer had to bear.

It was void of the spirit that made Stella who
    she was.
My friend on earth was no longer to be.
She now roams the great beyond
With no limits to her ability.

I can see her now as she flits here and there,
Unencumbered by such bodies as ours.
She can walk through the tulips, dance with
    daisies,
Or stoop to enjoy any flower.

I will continue to miss my best friend,
Until she's at the gate when my Lord calls
    me home.
She made such a difference in my life.
She is the best friend I have ever known.

99

OVER TIME

When a time in your life has brought you pain,
A friend stands firmly by your side.
Comforting you in your hurt,
While putting her own pain aside.

They take your hand and hold it,
Listening to each word you have to say.
Telling you to hold fast to Jesus,
Not letting the pain get in your way.

To never let anyone around you,
Cause any hurt to go so deep.
That you contemplate standing aside,
Letting Satan overcome your belief.

They help you to stand firm,
When darts are thrown your way.
Holding fast to the hand of Jesus,
Hoping He will make the truth known
    someday.

Now my friend is no longer here,
But she taught me how to be strong.
To stand firm in my belief of Jesus,
And over time He will right all wrongs.

FOREVER

Let go and let me have it.
It is not yours it is Mine.
I am in charge of what will be,
For your life and Mine are entwined.

I called you and you answered.
I looked into your eyes and I saw Myself.
I am your Lord and Master.
Me and no one else.

I took it upon Myself to save you.
I chose to pay a debt I did not owe.
And now that you are free from that debt,
You are unencumbered by life's earthly woes.

When you accepted the love I gave,
And you took Me into your heart,
I claimed you as My own,
And from you I will never depart.

I will be there through thick and thin.
I will be there forever and a day.
My love for you will never fail,
And by your side I will forever stay.

NEW JOURNEY

Lord I sit and await your arrival.
The time grows short for a loved one to go
   home.
She chose to give herself to You long ago,
For she knew You were the only One.

She saw You at a young age,
Immediately choosing You as her own.
She never once divvied from the path,
That took her to the Father by way
   of the Son.

She gave her love unconditionally.
A love in the truest of forms.
She mentored, guided and loved so many,
When they faced their own life's storm.

She gave of her love freely.
She had the ability to correct in a gentle way.
She pointed everyone in the right direction,
Never letting her love for Jesus go astray.

It's a gift some are given.
It's a gift many have sought.
It's a gift she did not even know she had.
It's a gift that cannot be bought.

Now she readies herself for a new journey.
One where there will be no pain at the end.
A journey that will find her sitting at the feet of Jesus
Gazing into the eyes of her best friend.

RELIEF

Moments of grief wash over me.
I don't even want to think,
But time presses on anyway,
And the days ahead seem dark and bleak.

I reach my hand out for comfort,
And immediately a nail-scarred hand appears.
I grab hold and hold on tightly,
While fighting hard to hold back tears.

I relax into Your arms as grief overcomes me.
It is then I find the most incredible peace.
The kind of peace that only Jesus can give.
It is in His arms I finally find relief.

Relief from the pain of loss.
Relief from the depth of my sorrow.
Relief in knowing You will take care of the
    days ahead,
As I place into Your hands all of my tomorrows.

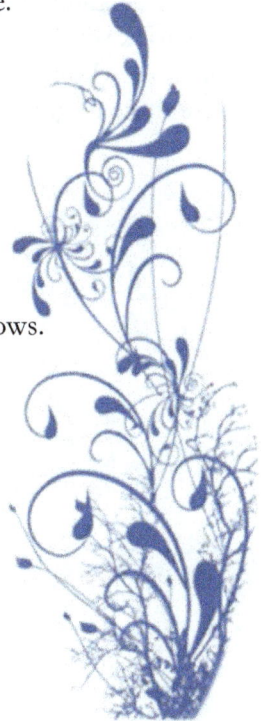

HEAVEN'S DOOR

I know you are in a better place.
You have now met Jesus face to face.
For when Jesus put forth His hand,
He took you home to the Promise Land.

A place where you can stand straight and tall.
Where you can skip through the tulips and not fall.
Jesus was there to welcome you home.
In a place filled with so much love and then some.

In the twinkling of an eye you were no longer here,
Jesus took you home amid shouts and cheers.
For those who had gone on before,
Were there to greet you as you stepped through
    Heaven's Door.

FINALITY

Today is a day of finality
For a loved one has gone home.
The mountains, hills and valleys
She never more will roam.

I can just see her now,
As she looks down from above.
Her body now free from all pain,
And a smile filled with so much love.

A love given to everyone she knew,
But a special love for her family.
It came with no ties that bind,
And it was given unconditionally.

We will miss her in the days ahead,
But there is one truth we can hold on to.
She is waiting for us to join her,
As she walks in the light of Heaven's
    morning dew.

YOU HAVE SOMEONE

When you lose someone you love,
The depth of sadness goes deep.
You feel as if you have lost part of yourself.
The days pass slowly and the nights allow you
   no sleep.

You go about your daily chores,
Doing each one only by rote.
Keeping busy by visiting family and friends,
Is what is keeping you a float.

At night when it all comes to an end,
And your mind has time to think.
Loneliness surrounds you in that moment,
And the future looks dark and bleak.

You have someone you can lean on.
Someone who will take your pain and give
   you peace.
Someone who will dry your tears,
As He lifts you from off your knees.

He will comfort you in the days ahead,
More than anyone else is able to do.
Cling to Him in your time of sorrow,
Letting His peace flow all over you.

TRIED BY GRACE

In times of testing, tragedy and sorrow,
We wonder why some survive and others do not.
The issues are so complex their significance escapes us,
But as human beings, that is our lot.

God has a plan for each individual one interwoven with
   so many lives,
One that contains past, present and future with so many
   options it boggles the mind.
There isn't a computer in this whole universe,
That can track the eternal dimensions of time.

When people tragically lose their lives,
Whether by evil or the fallen condition of man.
Their families and friends have the choice of
   succumbing to bitterness.
Or to grow in grace which is God's
   ultimate plan.

The issue is not what you can understand,
Or even tell yourself face to face.
The issue is to remember not to measure events by your
standards,
But to leave the consequences to be tried by grace.

SWEET BYE AND BYE

You listen, but hear no sound.
You search, but no one is there.
You roam the house in silence,
Then go down on your knees in prayer.

Some things are just too personal,
To share with anyone.
The hurt goes so deep inside of you,
You crave the presence of God's Son.

It is only in Him you find relief.
Night after night His presence you seek.
You let Him wrap His arms around you,
For it is only with Him you find sleep.

The days ahead will be filled with family
    and friends,
But then it is time for them to go home.
That's when the finality of what has happened,
    hits you,
And you know you must travel this road alone.

Hold fast to the hand of our Savior,
For He knows the pain you are going through.
He walked this world just as we.
He will wrap His arms around you.

He will give you His strength if you ask.
He will take you in His arms as you cry.
He will give you the peace that surpasses
    all understanding,
And someday you will join Him in the
    sweet bye and bye.

A place where there will be no more pain.
A place where your heart will feel no more sorrow.
So keep your eyes on the horizon.
And give Jesus all of your tomorrows.

Poems From the Heart

9781937911614 (soft cover)
9781937911621 (hard cover)
9781937911669 (ebook)

The decision to follow Jesus is the most important decision of your life. I pray that as you read the enclosed poems, they will cause you to seek a deeper relationship with Him.

She's Mine

9781937911614 (soft cover)
9781937911621 (hard cover)
9781937911669 (ebook)

Chloe kept trying to pull free, but the person that held her under the water had his hands entangled in her hair and she couldn't get away. Darkness threatened but still she tried. And then, nothing.

GOD Things

9781937911959 (soft cover)
9781937911966 (hard cover)

So as we go about our day,
And we give credit to the Lord above.
We find it is in all those little "God Things".
That we are woven together with His love.

Silent and Still

9781937911973 (soft cover)
9781937911980 (hard cover)
9781937911997 (ebook)

The man was already in place when the sun came up the next morning. He stood by his favorite tree smiling to himself as he watched the back of the house. He had come up with the most brilliant plan, or so he thought, and he couldn't wait to put it into action.

Meet the Author

La Johna Newbould

is a late-in-life Christian. It wasn't until she was in her early forties that she accepted Jesus Christ as her Lord and Savior. Once again she fills led to publish two more books. So with a total of four, she steps forward in faith, believing that anyone who reads any one of them will chose to have a relationship with Jesus, one step at a time. For everyone has to begin somewhere.

www.ingramcontent.com/pod-product-compliance
Lightning Source LLC
LaVergne TN
LVHW021714080426
835510LV00010B/997